For Barry Martin, in loving memory
—V. G.

*For Anne Tally and Charlie Saunders, who believed in me,
and Jeffrey Scales and Bob Ware, who taught me*
—J. I.

Henry Holt and Company, LLC, *Publishers since 1866*
175 Fifth Avenue, New York, New York 10010
www.HenryHoltKids.com

Henry Holt® is a registered trademark of Henry Holt and Company, LLC.
Text copyright © 2009 by Valerie Gladstone and Alvin Ailey Dance Foundation, Inc.
Ailey® and Alvin Ailey® are registered marks of Alvin Ailey Dance Foundation, Inc.
Photographs copyright © 2009 by José Ivey
All rights reserved.
Distributed in Canada by H. B. Fenn and Company Ltd.

Library of Congress Cataloging-in-Publication Data
Gladstone, Valerie.
A young dancer: the life of an Ailey student / Valerie Gladstone ; photographs by José Ivey. —1st ed.
p.   cm.
ISBN 978-0-8050-8233-3
1. Alvin Ailey American Dance Theater—Juvenile literature. 2. Ballet dancing—Juvenile literature.
[1. Alvin Ailey American Dance Theater.] I. Ivey, José, ill. II. Title.
GV1786.A42G53 2009   792.8'0973—dc22   2008018343

First Edition—2009 / Designed by Meredith Pratt
Printed in August 2009 in China by South China Printing Company Ltd.,
Dongguan City, Guangdong Province, on acid-free paper. ∞

3 5 7 9 10 8 6 4 2

A Young
DANCER

The Life of an **AILEY** Student

Valerie Gladstone

Photographs by JOSÉ IVEY

Christy Ottaviano Books
Henry Holt and Company
NEW YORK

My name is Iman Bright.

I started taking dance classes at The Ailey School in New York City when I was four years old. I'm thirteen now and in seventh grade. I go to a private school called Riverdale Country School. It's in the Bronx near the apartment complex where I live. I go to Ailey three days a week in the late afternoon. It takes a half hour on the Riverdale school bus to get there.

My school was founded by the great dancer and choreographer who started the Alvin Ailey American Dance Theater in 1958. Before then, there were very few companies that hired people of color. Mr. Ailey gave them an opportunity to dance and created beautiful dances for them to perform. The company is popular all over the world.

Ballet class begins with exercises at the barre in five different positions of the feet. I stay alert by concentrating on getting the steps right. That doesn't mean I always do. I mess up sometimes. Everybody does.

There are seven levels at The Ailey School, and the students in each level wear a different color. I'm a Level 5 and wear a burgundy leotard with pink tights and ballet slippers. In dance, you express feelings through movement. It's wonderful to have another way to express yourself besides words.

My room is my sanctuary. I put up photos of my friends and family on my bulletin board. I like to draw, especially plants and flowers. Right now, I'm not sure what I want to be when I grow up—a dancer or a graphic artist or maybe a violinist. I have about four hours of homework a night, which makes it pretty hard to squeeze everything in.

There's a reason for each exercise. Some are good for warming up and stretching our muscles, and others for teaching the positions that are basic to ballet.

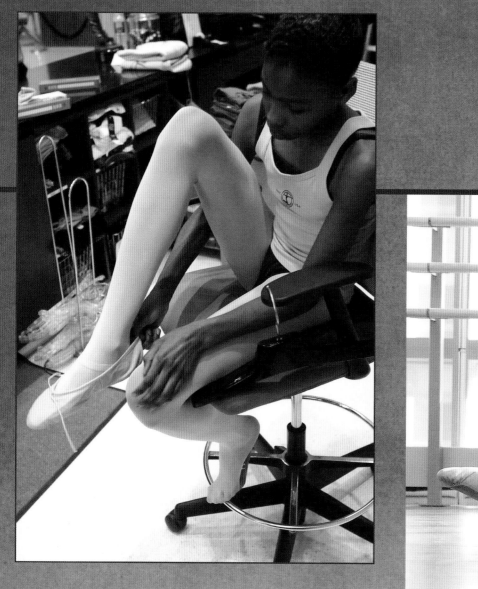

Ballet slippers have to fit just right.
I have long, thin feet, so it isn't easy
to find a pair that are comfortable.

When you're learning to do a split, you start slowly, easing just a little each time, and never forcing it. It took me years to get all the way down. Every night before I go to sleep, I extend my legs to keep in practice.

The Riverdale Country School is situated on almost twenty acres, so often there are long walks between classes. But it's great in nice weather when my friends Gaby and Amelia and I can go out on the sports fields at recess and make up dances. We've been studying Greek mythology, so one windy day we did a dance to the wind gods and chanted as we caught falling leaves.

We study different techniques, so that we'll be able to perform ballet, jazz, modern, and West African. In Horton, which is named for Alvin Ailey's mentor Lester Horton, the focus is on large, full movements.

In Limón, which is named for the choreographer José Limón, you concentrate on becoming more fluid in your movements. We learn West African dance from the countries of Mali and Guinea. West African dance is great for building stamina. I especially love jumping.

Miss Comendador tells me to hold my head high because that's in the ballet tradition. Ballet was first created to entertain kings and queens. When dancers performed, they were expected to keep their heads turned toward their direction. Now the audience takes the place of royalty, and we're supposed to treat it just as respectfully.

Every May the school holds a performance at a
nearby theater, and we can invite all our family
and friends. This year my level will perform a ballet
to the "Spring" section of Vivaldi's *The Four Seasons*
and a dance called *Ballet at Night Fall* using Limón
technique to wild Gypsy klezmer music. When we
begin rehearsals, I feel like a professional dancer.
It's my favorite time of year.

Actually, I just like being in a dance studio.

Aliymah and I have been friends since we
started at Ailey, so we talk about everything—
our families, teachers, music, TV, and movies.
I like having two sets of friends—one at my
regular school and the other at Ailey.

Ms. Jamison is the artistic director of Alvin Ailey American Dance Theater. She coached us in *Revelations*, Alvin Ailey's most famous dance, which is performed to spirituals. It's about hardship and survival. It makes me feel good, like I'm in church.

Ms. Jamison is considered one of the most famous members of the Ailey company. I've seen her dance in videos, and she is amazing.

She's very direct and funny when she gives corrections. In one part of the dance, she said I looked more like I was delivering groceries than proudly showing the way to God. A big difference.

For West African dance, we wear bright-colored wrap-around skirts, called *lappas*, and perform to drumming. The rhythms make me want to move.

My Limón teacher, Miss Steinman, corrects my posture during our warm-up exercises. You need strong stomach muscles to dance well, and the push-up position, called the plank, helps with that.

To be a good dancer, you should be able to pay attention, learn quickly, have lots of energy, and love dance. I think I have all those things.

We began learning the Limón dance three months before the performance in May. In the dance, we play guests at a Jewish wedding having a wonderful time.

Our pianist, Bill, accompanies the Límon classes. He improvises everything. It's much more fun to dance to real music than to recordings. But for our recital dances, we have to use recordings. Still, the music is so passionate, it feels live.

Sometimes my older sister, Tarika, brings my niece, Kheyana, to Ailey to pick me up after class. They ask a hundred questions about what I do here.

My mom takes me to my violin class on Saturday mornings before my afternoon dance class at Ailey. On the way, we stop for homemade soup. Usually, I eat healthfully, mostly fruits and vegetables. It makes a difference in how my body feels.

Dancing makes me feel free.

Miss Comendador
tells me that since my
legs are still growing I
have to be especially
aware of the changes
and make adjustments.

Studying violin helps my dancing. I play music by the same composers that we often dance to in ballet class, like Bach, Mozart, Vivaldi, and Tchaikovsky. I'll perform in Carnegie Hall in June with the orchestra from my violin school, School for Strings. Carnegie is one of the most famous concert halls in the world.

Jake is supposed to lift me
in the Limón dance, but
sometimes he just can't do it.

We all have different movements to perform as the wedding guests.

Miss Comendador made long, flowing skirts in pretty colors for the Limón dance.

I put gel on my hair and then pull it back so it's nice and smooth and the bun in the back isn't too big or too small.

We did Aliymah's hair for her.

Older dancers helped us get ready. It made me less nervous when they said, "I remember when I was like you, just starting out."

This is when we realize the importance of all
the classes and rehearsals and how exciting
it could be to be a professional dancer.

Being backstage, you can see all the details that go into a performance—the lighting and the sound and the dancers waiting to go onstage and then coming off exhilarated.

The first time I was onstage, I felt like smiling and laughing. Now I get completely caught up in the dance. Performing has given me much more self-confidence.

It's fun being onstage with your friends.

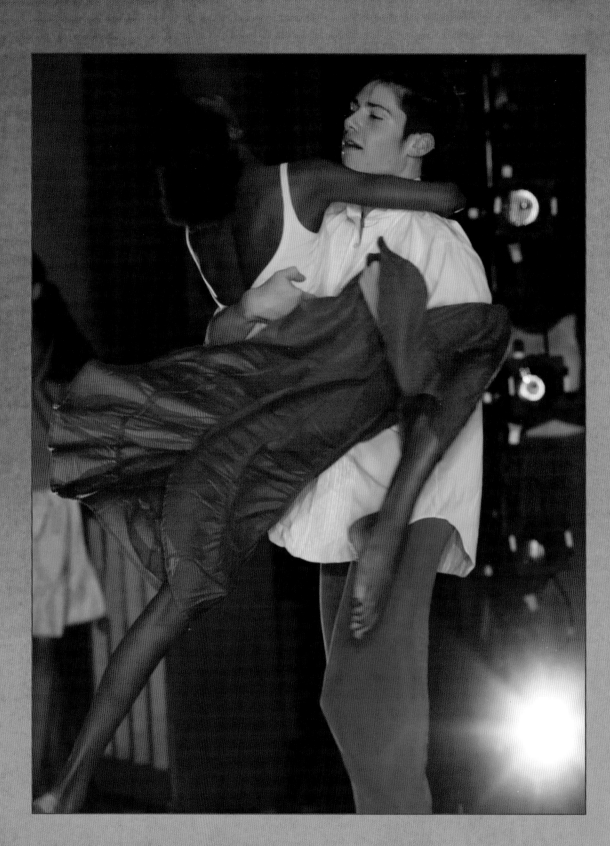

And this time, Jake caught me just right.

I didn't want the dance to end.

Mr. Sipp, dean of the Riverdale Middle School, came to the performance. It makes me feel special when people say how much they like the way I dance. Maybe I will be a dancer when I grow up.

This summer, I'll sleep in every morning and swim in the pool at my apartment complex. And in the fall, I will graduate to Level 6 and learn to dance even better.

Author's Note

The Alvin Ailey American Dance Theater grew out of a groundbreaking performance in March 1958, at the 92nd Street Young Men's Hebrew Association in New York City. Led by Alvin Ailey and a group of young African-American modern dancers, that event changed forever the perception of American dance. Today, the legacy continues with Artistic Director Judith Jamison's remarkable vision and the extraordinary artistry of the Company's dancers. The Company has performed for more than twenty-one million people in forty-eight states and in seventy-one countries on six continents and has earned a reputation as one of the most acclaimed international ambassadors of American culture, promoting the African-American cultural experience and the preservation and enrichment of American modern dance heritage.

Guided by the belief that dance instruction should be made available to everyone, Mr. Ailey founded a school in 1969, with an initial enrollment of 125 students. Today, The Ailey School is flourishing, and a faculty of dance professionals trains more than three thousand aspiring dancers annually in the Junior Division and full-time Professional Division, which includes a Bachelor of Fine Arts degree program in conjunction with Fordham University. Ailey II serves as a bridge between the school and the professional dance world. In addition, The Ailey Extension was launched in 2005 to provide dance and fitness classes for the general public.

In December 2004, the Alvin Ailey American Dance Theater, Ailey II, and The Ailey School moved to a permanent home at 405 West 55th Street in Manhattan—the Joan Weill Center for Dance—the largest facility dedicated to dance in the United States.

For more information, visit www.alvinailey.org. To find a dance school, go to http://dancemagazine.com/dancefinder or http://dancemagazine.com/dad.